Samoa

Talofa   greeting of love

Samoa
A Photographic Essay

Frederic Koehler Sutter

Introduction by Peter Pirie

Honolulu   THE UNIVERSITY PRESS OF HAWAII

Library of Congress Catalog Card Number 74-168975
All rights reserved by The University Press of Hawaii
(formerly University of Hawaii Press, ISBN 0-87022-778-5)
Manufactured in the United States of America

Designed by John C. Nye

First printing 1971
Second printing 1975
Third printing 1979

Dedicated to the people of Western Samoa

Ia Samoa peleina: fa'afetai mo lo 'outou agalelei, fa'afetai mo lo 'outou agaalofa.

and to my wife Sharon
and daughter Lisenga

Contents

Preface	ix
Introduction	xi
Prologue	2
The People	8
The Village Day Begins	12
Women's Work	18
Men's Work	24
Children at Work and Play	46
Ceremonies and Celebrations	54
Religion	64
Evening	70
Epilogue	74
Notes	80
Proverbs Cited	92

Preface

When my wife and I first came to Western Samoa in 1962, we wanted to record and share the lives of the people among whom we were living. Photography proved the most appealing medium, and the one with which I felt the most success.

In the book which follows, I have tried to present the people of Samoa, their culture, and their islands as I have seen and experienced them. The photo essay was conceived of as a day in Samoa—in actuality a composite of many places and days—as it is lived by the chiefs, pastors, men, women, and children.

Several themes are interwoven. The village day from sunrise through nightfall is shown; so too is the cycle of life—childhood, youth, adulthood, old age, and death. Also, within the context of the physical setting shown in the Prologue, the reader can see the social environment and the patterns of culture unfold in the divisions of labor, status, and responsibility. These patterns are reinforced when all parts of the society unite in ceremonies, celebrations, and religious life. These special events and the proverbial sayings accompanying many of the photographs recall the wisdom and tradition of Samoan history and reveal a stability and continuity through time that fuses past and present. The Epilogue gives a last glimpse of these people, their lives and land, their traditions and their future.

For the most part, I have tried to use proverbs and sayings as captions. These represent a distillation of Samoan culture over the centuries and offer great insight into the values and thoughts which underlie the Samoan way of life. The proverbs are first given in Samoan, followed by a fairly literal English translation. Where this is not sufficient, the wider application is suggested.

In selecting the proverbs, I have drawn on the collections made by Dr. E. Schultz in 1906 as translated and amplified by Brother Herman (*Proverbial Expressions of the Samoans*, Polynesian Paperbacks No. 1, Polynesian Society, Wellington, N.Z., 1965), and on compilations by the Reverend George Brown ("Proverbs, Phrases, and Similes of the Samoans," *Report of the Fourteenth Meeting of the Australasian Association for the Advancement of Science*, Sydney, 1914), and by the Reverend George Pratt (*Pratt's Grammar and*

Dictionary of the Samoan Language, 4th ed., J. E. Newell, ed., Malua, Western Samoa: Malua Printing Press, 1960). Finally, I am most grateful for the advice and assistance of Etene Sa'aga and numerous Samoan friends in the translation and usage of these proverbs.

Over the past seven years, many people have assisted me in creating this book. I am especially indebted to my wife Sharon, for her inspiration and untiring help; my parents, the Reverend Dr. and Mrs. Carl J. Sutter, my grandmother, Mrs. Dora Koehler, and my dear friend, Mrs. Elsbeth Bayerdorffer, have provided me with continuous encouragement and support. My thanks, too, to my son Uele.

In Samoan, courtesy and respectful regard are expressed in the word *fa'aaloalo*. It is a highly esteemed characteristic of Samoan custom. This word has been personified for me in the Reverend Safa'i Tupe and his wife Ta'ase, with whom I have lived while in the village of Satoalepai and who have always extended to me their gracious hospitality and care. Mr. and Mrs. Robert Lincoln Batchelor of Apia, the Ala'ilima family of Samoa and Hawaii, and the Reverend Mr. and Mrs. Fa'afouina Iofi of Honolulu have given both friendship and assistance.

A word of thanks cannot express my gratitude to my friend Faletolu Tavita, who accompanied me on many photographic expeditions and helped, rain or shine, night or day. Finally, to all those people who enjoyed seeing the photographs and suggested that they might be combined into a book, my appreciation: Robert I. Levy, Ab and Syl Hurwitz, Peter and Avis Pirie, Renee Heyum, and Bo and Birgitta Dahlborg.

Thank you all, for your suggestions, encouragement, and support.

F. K. S.
Satoalepai, Savai'i
Western Samoa

Introduction

Contact between Samoans and *papalagi,* the foreigners from Atlantic shores, began in 1722 when Roggeveen, a Dutch navigator, first found their islands as he sailed eastward across the Pacific. His description of the discovery was not informative. Although thousands have visited the island group since, and many distinguished writers and scholars have set themselves the task of portraying Samoa and its people, much remains yet to be told, and of all the Pacific peoples the Samoans remain to the outside world among the more baffling and enigmatic.

Rick Sutter's approach to the Samoans and their islands is one that has not been tried before. He combines the refined technique and quick eye of the expert photographer with the perception and sensitivity of the field anthropologist. Along with the familiar photographic concept of "peak action," he has been able, in his choice of pictures, to capture a rarer quality, "peak culture," for Rick Sutter sees these Polynesians of today surely as they would like to see themselves. Little intrudes that is not *fa'a Samoa.* To know Samoa well and to look at his pictures is to experience repeated shocks of recognition. For the stranger to Samoa, his pictures must combine to leave the impression of a people who, although they have absorbed many foreign institutions, have continued nevertheless to remain very much themselves. Samoan life now relates to the Christian churches, to a formal school system, to a parliamentary government, and to Anglo-Saxon law as much as to its older institutions, but to each adoption they have affixed their own distinctive stamp.

The Samoans are shown in this book as a rural, village-dwelling, agricultural people, oriented to tradition, to ceremonial, to respect for the Samoan way. The tourist who arrives only with this idyllic vision, and who then confines himself to Apia, the capital city, may be in for some surprises; but in the villages, where over two-thirds of all Samoans still live, the picture is a true one. Rick Sutter has used his lens to convey those complexities within a culture that are not always readily discernible. The child is pictured as burdened with his work, his younger relatives, his school, and his need to serve and defer to his elders. The young man is shown grappling with cash crop agriculture, growing subsistence food for his family, harvesting the coral reef on which the fish get scarcer, roaming the Pacific Ocean in search of the increasingly elusive bonito, or enduring the tattoo. At the same time he is feeling the evermore compelling need to assert himself socially, sexually, and politically. One picture, "the whispering of chiefs" suggests, in a momentary glimpse of a facial expression, the tensions of village and national politics. These are the prerogative only of the matai, the holders of the family title, but to the traditional maneuverings for prestige have been added the complexities and risks of administration. By identifying and recording the revealing moment, and by deft selection, Rick Sutter, through these photographs, draws us into some understanding of how it is now to be a Samoan.

He has employed ingeniously some of the traditional sayings of the Samoans to explain and link his pictures. In their speechmaking and even in conversation Samoans tend to be very allusive. Many of their sayings are little more than catchphrases. They have added to their own sayings translations of many proverbs and sayings of the *papalagi*, particularly from the Bible. Their own more authentic aphorisms, however, tend to suggest that the Samoan view of life contrasts sharply with that shared by the English-speaking cultures. For instance, few mothers could be persuaded to echo the Samoan mother's conventional wish for her child "may he grow in a swamp" before it was pointed out to her that the allusion is to the taro, the Samoan's main subsistence food crop which grows best in constantly moist soil. On a more profound level, the concept "may the best man win" is one deeply embedded in our competitive culture, but the Samoan answers with "my turn today, yours tomorrow." The English-speaking peoples tend to treat mere words rather lightly. Their proverbs suggest, for instance, that "words are but wind," "words are but sands, but 'tis money buys lands," "fine words butter no parsnips," and "hard words break no bones" (although we do recognize that in some circumstances "the pen is mightier than the sword"). The Samoan treats the spoken word more reverently; he says, "stones rot, but words last forever." These contrasts in conventional folk wisdom point up the difficulties of cross-cultural negotiation. The problems are of some magnitude, for, as with experience the *papalagi* comes to perceive—if he begins to understand at all—the conventional Samoan view of life is in most ways the opposite, and even the reciprocal, of his own. Within the *papalagi fa'a Samoa*, among whom Rick Sutter must certainly be counted, this situation has given rise to an activity, amounting almost to a parlor game, in which topics of the folk wisdom of the West are reinterpreted and rephrased in the Samoan way. One example here must suffice: "the camera never lies" is a statement which, though obviously modern, is attaining the stature of an English proverb. But a Samoan might say instead "the shutter must click a thousand times before one truth is caught." It would be difficult to decide, under the circumstances, which expresses the better insight. But it will be obvious to anyone who browses this book that Rick Sutter, in his selections chosen from many thousands of pictures, has demonstrated along with the technical arts of good photography his skills in cross-cultural sensitivity and his perception on the other side of the lens among the Samoans.

Peter Pirie

Samoa

The four main islands of Western Samoa...

Prologue

are volcanic in origin

The fringing reefs form wide lagoons...

edged by beaches.

Ia lafoia i le alogalu. May you be cast on the far side of the reef. *Proverb: May you overcome all difficulties*

High mountains drain the clouds

Ua aofia i le futiafu e tasi. All becomes one in the basin of the waterfall. *Proverb.*

Sa matou tu'u la'au mai nei. We have rested un[der] many trees on our way here. *Proverb: On our journ[ey] we have enjoyed much hospital[ity.]*

Tolona e le masina matua. Clouds swept away by the full grown moon. *Proverb referring to the advice of an old man in times of trouble.*

Ua solo le lāvalima. The braiding of the coconut twine is proceeding rapidly. *Proverb: Favorable progress indicates eventual success.*

eople

'O le isi le momo'o. Praising is asking. *Proverb.*

Ua pulapula a la goto. Like the glow of the setting sun. *Compliment to old people.*

faiva ʻaulelei. Only a handsome man can do a
ing well. *Proverb.*

The Village Day Begins

Ua sanisani fa'amanuao. The joy of the welcome is like birds greeting the dawn. *Proverb.*

Taule'ale'a usu mai. Young men who go to their families in the early morning. *Words of praise.*

Smoke from the ground ovens fills the morning air.

Each village has its trader's shop.

The ear makes a convenient purse.

Na o le taeao o faiva. One should go fishing only i the morning. *Proverb: Early morning is th best time for wor*

Women's Work

Dried coconut meat, copra, is an important cash crop.

Shaving the lawn with a bush knife.

E tasi 'ae afe. Only one but worth a thousand. *Compliment recalling a beautiful fine mat, applied to outstanding character.*

The *fuataga*, a festival celebrating the completion of fine-mat weaving

LEFT: Decorating the women's committee house.
T: Printing tapa cloth made from the bark
he paper mulberry.

Ia tupu i se fusi. May he grow in a swamp. *Humble prayer that one's child will thrive as does a food plant in moist soil.*

These young men await their chiefs' work allocations.

Men's Work

Ia lua'i lou le 'ulu taumamao. Gather the most distant breadfruit first. *Proverb.*

Ua vela lana umu i lo tatou nu'u. In our village his ground oven is done. *Compliment to a man whose good qualities and hard work make him an asset to his village.*

Ua tofo i tino matagi lelei. A favorable wind is felt on the body. *Proverb: The joy of expectation.*

Māmā i avega si'i. The light weight of a burden when first lifted. *Proverb.*

Fā le taeao e le afiafi. He who sits at home in the morning will not have food in the evening. *Prover*

Mālō le 'onosa'i. Congratulations to patience. *Saying.*

O le i'a a tautai e alu i le fa'alolo. The fish seem to do the will of the chief fisherman. *Expression of obedience.*

Ja penapena i tua o tai i'a. They were too late for ne palolo. *Proverb: He who comes late must be ontent with what is left.*

Ua aʻe aʻe lea manu ua ulu. The bird surfaces with a good catch. *Proverb.*

Faʻatoetoe le muli o le ola. Save the remainder of the basket for others. *Proverb.*

O le upega e tautau, 'ae fagota. The net is now drying, but it will soon be wet again. *An exhortation not to despair.*

O le fa'afiti a tautai. The denial of a fisherman. *Proverb said of someone who disavows possession of what he wants to keep.*

Ua logo le na i ama, logo le na i atea. He feels a bite on both sides of the canoe. *Proverb expressing joy over a task successfully completed.*

Preparation for shark lassooing.
O le malie ma le tuʻu malie. Each shark caught has its payment.
Proverb applied to killing or kindness.

fili i le tai se agavaʻa. Let the sea determine the quality of the noe. *Proverb referring to misfortune as a test of friendship.*

O upu matatutupa. Words without points. *Proverb.*

Ua sau le va'a na tiu tau mai i le va'a na tau. The boat that went fishing came home and met the boat that stayed on shore. *Proverb. Words of gratitude said on arriving home safely and finding everyone well.*

38

Ua logo 'ese'ese fa'amea vilivili. Holes bored from opposite sides frequently do not meet. *Proverb said of a meeting of chiefs where differing opinions cannot be reconciled.*

Ia ta'amilo pea ma tautala. The house can be turned—the lashings will hold. *Proverb: After mature reflection, it is safe to act.*

Ia oloolo pitova'a. Let each one smooth his part of the boat. *Proverb: Attend to your own affairs; don't meddle.*

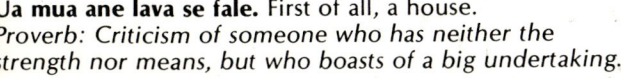
Weaving the thatch.

Ua mua ane lava se fale. First of all, a house.
Proverb: Criticism of someone who has neither the strength nor means, but who boasts of a big undertaking.

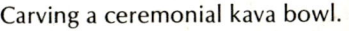
Carving a ceremonial kava bowl.

Pula ū. Tasteless taro. *Saying about a man who has no tattoo.*

O āu tatau. The tattooing combs.

Tuʻufau, mai aliʻi ē!	Relax, O Sir!
ʻAʻo le tu mai ea a le vavau.	This is an old-time custom.
Te saga oi oe, ʻa e pese aʻu:	You groan continually, but I sing
E tupu le fafine fanau,	The woman must bear children,
E tupu le tane tā le tatau...	The man must be tattooed...

Tattoo song.

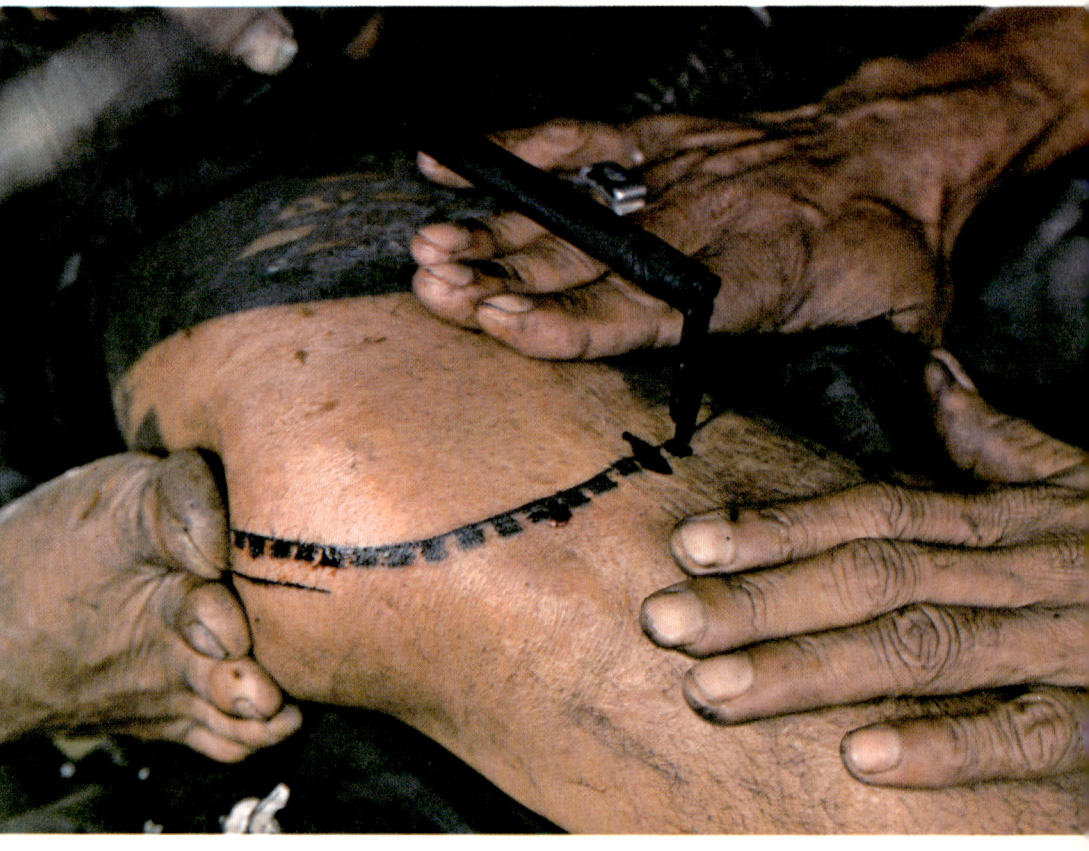

Fepaʻiaʻi le ʻau ma le sāusāu, The chisel and hammer strike,
Molia le lama, ʻina tau ... The color is laid on so that it sticks ...

Tattoo song.

E isia le 'ula, isia le fau,
'Ae le isia si au tatau,
'O si au ula tutumau,
E te alu ma oe i le tu'ugamau.

The necklace breaks, the cord breaks,
But your tattoo does not break into pieces,
This, your necklace, is lasting,
And goes with you to the grave.

Tattoo song.

Children, wearing their village school uniforms, bring flowers each morning to decorate their classrooms.

Morning prayer—too early.

Children at Work and Play

Ua leai se ulu e ala. There is not even time to scratch one's head. *Proverb.*

Bringing kava sticks to a celebration.

E pala ma'a, 'ae le pala 'upu. Stones rot, but words last forever. *Proverb.*

Ceremonie

Preparing the "king's kava."

Ua le po malaē. On the meeting ground one feels as in a dark night. *Proverb.*

nd Celebrations

E oʻu le asō; ʻae o oe taeao. Today my turn; tomorrow yours. *Proverb.*

Musumusu a puialiʻi. The whisperings of chiefs. *Saying.*

Collecting and redistributing fine mats.

In the evening there are songs and dances.

Ua vela le fala. The mat is warm. *Proverb applied to a long dance or meeting.*

Once a year, the whole country joins together in celebrating Western Samoa's independence.

A *taupou*, titled hostess of the village.

Ua liua le tua ma le alo. The back is turned and then the front. *Saying of a man sent on many messages.*

Smoke from the ground ovens rises over Apia dawn; the village longboats race to shor

Religion

Announcing a church meeting.

A village church.

Ia uluulu matāfolau. To go from house to house.
Proverb applied to the Holy Spirit going from heart to heart.

Fa'avae i le Atua Samoa. Samoa is founded upon God.
Motto of the Independent State of Western Samoa.

Pastor's School: a child's first formal education

66

...rning to read the Bible. (above right)

Children's Sunday.

Ua felāta'i le la ma le sami. The sun and the sea are nearing each other. *Proverb.*

O le la'au e tu, 'ae ōia. The tree stands but it is marked for the woodsman. *Proverb.*

Ua tagi le fatu ma le eleʻele.
The stones and the earth wept. *Proverb.*

Tagi o alisi. The crying of crickets.
Reference to twilight.

Families gather for evening prayers.

Evening

Tāla lua Tuna ma Fata. Pray for both Tuna and Fat
Proverb: Do not restrict your love to only one perso

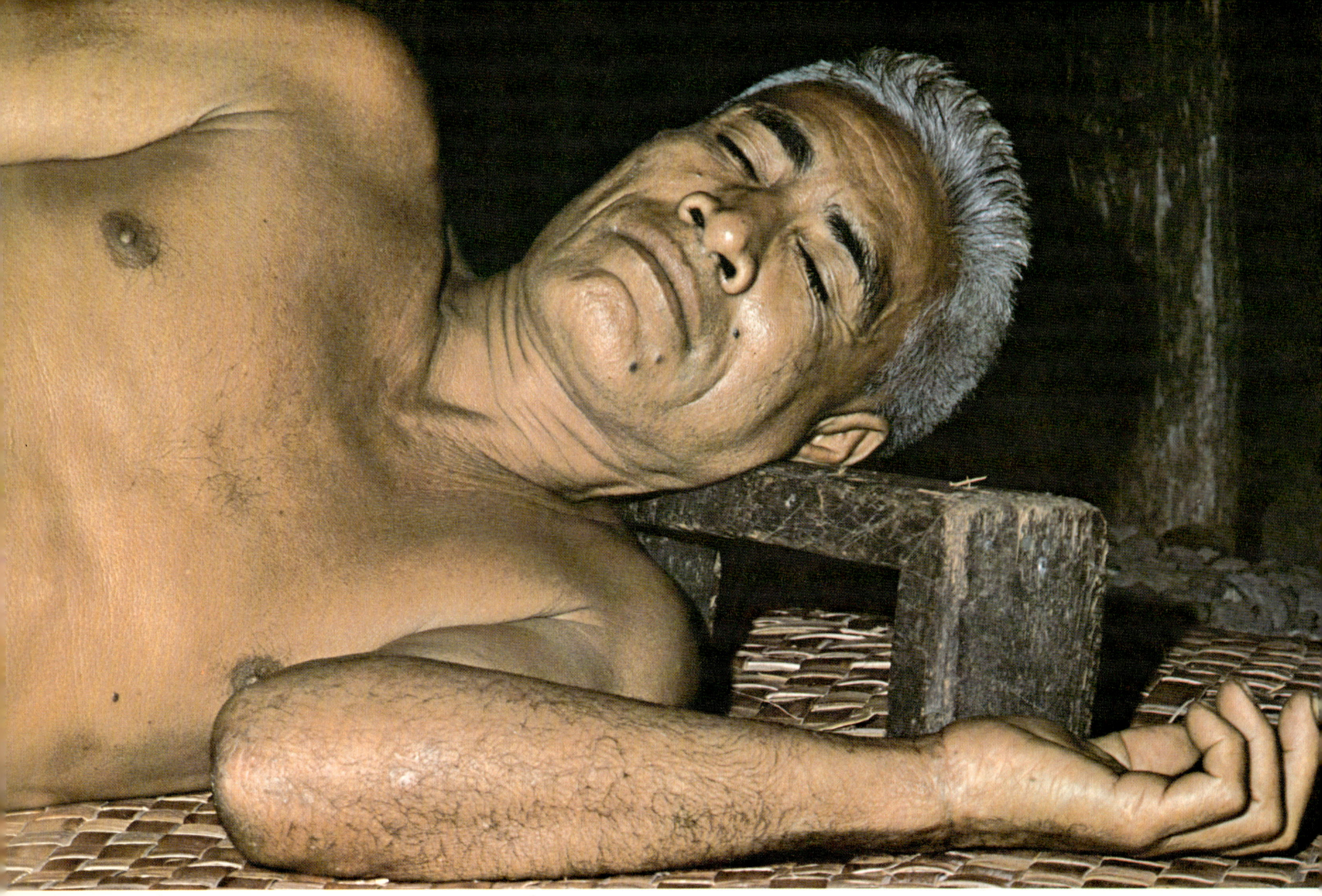

Ua tofa i vai, 'ae ala i 'ai. One can go to sleep with only a drink of water when one has the hope of awakening to a good meal. *Proverb: When the present is difficult, there is always hope for the future.*

The Southern Cross.

Samoa e le galo atu. O Samoa! I never will forget you. *Samoan farewell song.*

Epilogue

Ua leai se manu e ōlo. Not a pigeon is cooing. *Saying of a village where perfect peace reigns.*

Ua lāolāo le sami. The sea is smooth.
Proverb: Difficulties are gone; all is reconciled.

oi afā ma maninoa. The hurricane and
calm are neighbors. *Proverb.*

O le mavaega nai le tai e fetaia'i i i'u o gafa. The last farewell at the seashore, with the promise...

to meet again in the children. *Proverb*

Notes

PAGE ii. Singing Samoan youth playing his ukulele on the church steps epitomizes the spirit of *talofa*, greeting of love. [Satoalepai, Savai'i]

TITLE PAGE. The naming of Samoa lies in events of long ago recalled in the legend of Lu. Lu had a preserve of tabooed chickens, *sa moa*. One day the taboo was violated, and Lu made war against the offending family. Nearly devastating them, he chased them to the ninth heaven, where the high god, Tagaloa, interceded, warning that strife was forbidden in the tenth heaven. To appease Lu, Tagaloa offered his daughter in marriage. Peace was restored and the couple's first son was named Samoa, in memory of the sacred chickens of his father. Samoa was the progenitor of the family of Moa, *Sa Moa*, who became the kings of the island group.

Prologue

The islands of Western Samoa lie in the South Pacific halfway between Australia and Hawaii. All of the islands are volcanic in origin, and in some areas barren fields of lava from more recent eruptions stand in sharp contrast to the surrounding verdure. There is overall a lush greenness, the result of high annual rainfall, tropical temperatures, and fertile soil.

PAGE 2. The island of Upolu, foreground, is the most populous of the four principal islands of Western Samoa. The 6,000-foot mountains of distant Savai'i dwarf the smaller islands of Manono and Apolima. [western end of Upolu]

PAGE 3. The most recent volcanic eruptions occurred on Savai'i between 1905 and 1911. [Saleaula, Savai'i]

PAGE 4. *Top.* The reef-fringed lagoon stretches southward toward a crescent of uninhabited offshore islands, (clockwise from top left) Nu'ulua, Nu'utele, Namua, and Fanuatapu, used primarily by fishermen and as a source of coconuts and wild goats and cattle. The wide lagoon provides a sheltered and rich fishing ground. [eastern tip of Upolu]
Bottom. Beaching bonito canoes on Nu'utele during a fishing expedition. This island, once the site of a leprosarium, is now known for its turtle-nesting grounds. [Nu'utele, Aleipata, Upolu]

PAGE 5. In many parts of the island group, fringing reefs protect the shore from the open swells of the Pacific. [Apia, Upolu]

PAGE 6. *Left.* The heavy rainfall in the mountains filters through the porous volcanic rock or runs off in streams and rivers. Waterfalls can be found in almost every gorge. [Sopoaga Falls, Upolu]
Right. Many of the mountains, jagged and precipitous, reach several thousand feet in height. Precipitation averages 110 inches per year in the coastal areas and increases with the elevation. The abundance of water produces exuberant growth. Tradewinds which blow most of the year make the climate mild and equable. [Mt. Fao, Upolu]

PAGE 7. Inland from the villages and the cleared areas of family plantations lies the forest—a source of firewood, timber, wild pigs, and birds. [interior of Savai'i]

The People

Samoans are one of the most numerous of the Polynesian peoples. Their language and strong culture have developed over more than two thousand years.

Their large, extended families are led by matai, chiefs, who are responsible for organizing and managing the resources of the family. The matai of each family meet regularly in council to decide village affairs.

In 1966 the population of the country was about 134,000. Nearly 100,000 of the people live in rural areas where they farm the land behind their villages and fish the lagoons and open sea.

PAGE 8. *Top.* An aged talking chief, a *tulafale*, carries the symbols of his position, the staff and the flywhisk. [Papa, Sataua, Savai'i]
Right. A young talking chief. During village council deliberations, chiefs braid sennit, often called the "Samoan nail," from coconut-husk fibers. [Satoalepai, Savai'i]

PAGE 9. *Left.* Old ladies, called *lo'o matua*, are honored in Samoa, particularly for their knowledge of family genealogy. [Lalomanu, Upolu]
Top. A young woman of Samoa. She and other women of the village are members of the women's committee, which, among other things, helps with the care of village guests and assists in village health programs. [Lalomanu, Upolu]

PAGE 10. A young Samoan family. On the average, a couple in Samoa will have six children. Close ties between friends and relatives are strengthened by the adoption of each other's children. [Safa'i, Savai'i]

PAGE 11. *Top left.* A *taule'ale'a*, untitled man. *Taulele'a* is the term used for untitled men as a group. This category of men is often referred to as the "muscle of Samoa" because they perform much of the heavy work. In each village, the untitled men belong to a group called the *aumaga*, which provides a communal work force and participates in village social affairs of other kinds. [Asau, Savai'i]
Top right. A young girl. Until they are married, girls are in charge of rearing their younger brothers and sisters. [Satoalepai, Savai'i]
Bottom left and right. Children of Samoa. [Satufia, Savai'i, and Leulumoega, Upolu]

The Village Day Begins

The village stirs with the morning sun. People, wrapped in sheets to keep warm in the cool morning air, gradually awaken.

The heavy work of the day is done in the morning before the sun gets hot, and by ten or eleven, each family gathers for its first meal.

An average village is made up of about a score of large families. Practically every one of the twenty or so members of a family, from the toddlers to the elderly, helps with the work of the day.

PAGE 12. The sun is the alarm clock of Samoa. Its morning rays filter through the coconut-leaf blinds of the houses to announce the beginning of a new day. Samoans usually go to bed early and rise with the sun; but on the nights of the full moon, young people often stay up late to sing and walk in the moonlight. [Faleolo, Upolu]

PAGE 13. This little boy, still asleep under his mosquito net, will soon be up and about his chores. [Satoalepai, Savai'i]

PAGE 14. *Top.* In villages which have no waterline and tap, children are sent to collect water from the river. [Sili, Savai'i]
Right. Samoans usually bathe two or more times a day, a habit acquired early in life. [Leulumoega, Upolu]

PAGE 15. *Left.* Branches of a family are oftentimes scattered throughout a village. When a ground oven is opened, portions of the hot food are taken to nearby relatives. [Satufia, Savai'i]
Right. Ground ovens are usually made every other day. At other times, the food is boiled or fried over the fire. Customarily, the people eat a mid-morning and an evening meal. [Neiafu, Savai'i]

PAGE 16. *Left.* Each family earns cash by selling its bananas, dried coconut, and cocoa to the village trader. In turn they purchase cloth, kerosene, lanterns, sugar, and a few other items. For the most part, however, the villagers could manage to live without imported items. [Lotofaga, Upolu]
Right. The everyday wraparound lavalava, worn by both men and women, has no pockets. [Satufia, Savai'i]

PAGE 17. Both wash and cocoa beans dry in the morning sun. [Foālalo, Savai'i]

Women's Work

Village women do a great deal of work, much of it by hand. The only machine they commonly use is the manual sewing machine.

Most of their time is spent in and near their homes, where they tend the infants, keep the house, and do the wash at the tap or in the river. They help with weeding and other plantation work. Women supervise the older girls in the care of small children, and usually do the less strenuous cooking such as preparing the boiled soups, stews, and other foods, and making cocoa and tea. Still other work includes shellfishing, preparing herb medicines, and giving massage.

Women weave many types of mats and baskets, and make tapa cloth, having prepared the materials themselves. Their main entertainment is in visiting, working with, and helping one another.

PAGE 18. Early in the day, the women spread pieces of coconut meat on mats in the sun. Even when about their other work, they keep an eye on the weather lest the rain damage the copra. [Safa'i, Savai'i]

PAGE 19. *Top left.* Coconuts, which the men have harvested, are cut and spread in the sun to dry. Copra, dried coconut meat, is the major source of income; it enables a family to buy from the trader, pay the children's school expenses, and put something in the Sunday offering. [Safa'i, Savai'i]
Top right. A girl does the dishes beside her father's outrigger canoe. [Papa, Sataua, Savai'i]
Bottom left. Bushknives are used to cut the grass. It has been said that some villages are so beautifully kept they resemble parks. [Satoalepai, Savai'i]
Bottom right. A little girl watches admiringly as her older sister works the family sewing machine. A woman is expected to be able to make all the family clothing, and to do so without patterns. [Satoalepai, Savai'i]

PAGE 20. *Left.* A young girl learns to weave by watching an older woman in her family. [Satoalepai, Savai'i]
Center. On a given day each week, the women gather to weave fine mats, *ie toga*. A truly fine *ie toga* will have the consistency of linen, and may take as long as six years to weave. These mats are exchanged on those occasions of major significance in life, such as weddings, funerals, and the assumption of a title. They are also used as payment for the work of specialists in carpentry or tattooing. [Satoalepai, Savai'i]
Right. The bleached and dried pandanus leaves are split into thin strips, which are then woven on the diagonal. Extra fibers are added as needed. When completed the mat will be about six feet long and eight feet wide, measured in handspans. The last step is the addition of colorful bird feathers. [Satoalepai, Savai'i]

PAGE 21. When the women of the village have completed the weaving of a large number of fine mats, a celebration is held. The new mats are paraded and a feast and dancing follow. [Papa, Sataua, Savai'i]

PAGE 22. *Left.* Each day young women of the village take turns decorating the women's committee house with hibiscus and plumeria (frangipani) blossoms threaded onto the ribs of coconut fronds. Frequently this house is located near a freshwater pool, which is divided into drinking, bathing, and washing sections. Thus, the women at work in the committee house are able to supervise the use of the pool. [Satufia, Savai'i]
Top. Tapa cloth, *siapo*, is made from the inner layer of bark of young paper mulberry trees. The fibers are scraped and beaten until they gradually spread. Several layers are then pieced together. The white tapa, placed over boards carved by the men, is then ready for printing. [Satoalepai, Savai'i]
Bottom. Powdered ochre and dye extracted from a forest tree are rubbed across the tapa until the pattern emerges. Additional designs are painted on later with a pandanus-seed brush dipped in natural dyes or lampblack. *Siapo* are also ceremonial items of exchange. [Lalomanu, Upolu]

PAGE 23. The women's committee meets frequently. Each member wears the uniform decided upon by the group. The district nurse makes periodic rounds to inspect the children's health, weigh the babies, and give immunizations and talks. [Satoalepai, Savai'i]

Men's Work

The work of men includes farming, fishing, and working with wood. Each of these types of work requires both great strength and a number of skills, including the ability to make most of the needed tools.

Usually men and youths perform the heavy task of making the ground oven; they also do much of the ceremonial cooking. Men help tend the babies, and frequently take a child with them while they work.

Although a man can build his own house and boat with the help of his family, and boys make little tattoos on one another, there are also men who are experts in these types of work, and whose services are obtained for important projects.

The work of the family is organized and supervised by the matai. Every family possesses a title, which it almost always awards to one of its men, who then represents the dignity and honor of the family in the village council and other social affairs. Each matai, like all able-bodied men in the village, performs a share of the work.

PAGE 24. Usually, youths work their own family's land. In this picture, the *aumaga* receives instructions from the council of chiefs because the men are to work together to gather food for a village ceremony. [Sili, Savai'i]

PAGE 25. *Left.* Breadfruit ripen three or four times a year. The fruit is picked by twisting the stem with a long forked pole. A younger brother or sister below catches the falling fruit in a basket. [Leulumoega, Upolu]
Right. Once the nutritious root of the taro has been dug up, it is placed in the food basket and covered with the plant's edible tender leaves. A digging stick is used to make a hole in which the stem will be replanted. [Samalaeulu, Savai'i]

PAGE 26. *Left.* Most families have a papaya tree growing near their home. The fruit is eaten raw or made into a soup. [Safa'i, Savai'i]
Right. Weighed down with more than a hundred pounds of coconuts, a young man and his friend return home with a treasure. The meat can be made into copra to sell at the trader's shop, or into coconut cream for cooking; the husk may be used as fuel; the fibers can be braided into twine. Coconuts can be turned into scores of useful things. [Papa, Sataua, Savai'i]

PAGE 27. Carrying the day's harvest, a family wades through a sea of green—their plantation of taro and *ta'amu* (edible starchy roots). [Samalaeulu, Savai'i]

PAGE 28. Those who don't work the lands harvest the sea. One special kind of fishing occurs just before dawn on the sixth to eighth day after the full moon in October or November, when the palolo worms (*Eunice veridis*) rise from the reef. Samoans consider palolo a great delicacy and many come for the rising to those villages known to have an abundance. Draped with flowers to welcome these annually awaited visitors, the people quickly scoop them up before they melt in the morning light. [Satufia, Savai'i]

PAGE 29. *Left.* Wearing goggles and holding their spears and shanghais (rubber slings), two fishermen chat while waiting for high tide and word from the *tautai*, master fisherman, that it is time to begin spear fishing. One wears the intricately patterned traditional tattoo, which emphasizes the contours of his body. Frequently the men of the village fish in a group. Communal fishing is conducted regularly on Saturdays in preparation for the Sunday feast, held after the morning church service and shared by the chiefs and village pastor and then by their families. [near Manase, Savai'i]
Right. A *tautai* points to a new fishing ground. From his elevated position in the boat, he is able to sight new schools of fish. [Lalomanu, Upolu]

PAGE 30. *Top.* A handsomely tattooed spear fisherman peers beneath a coral ledge at a fish he frightened into hiding by slapping the surface of the water with his spear. This is the most common method of fishing and is practiced primarily in the lagoon. [Lalomanu, Upolu]
Bottom. An undersea hunter captures a turtle, a chiefly food. [Satoalepai, Savai'i]
Right. A fisherman surfaces with a *faisua*, large clam, found on the ocean floor thirty feet below. [Satoalepai, Savai'i]

PAGE 31. A basket of fish, which will be distributed among relatives and friends, waits on the shore while the canoe is beached. [Lalomanu, Upolu]

PAGE 32. *Left.* Delighted by the prospect of a tasty meal, a boy carries his father's catch. [Lotofaga, Upolu]
Right. Wearing girdles of their catch, spear fishermen head home from the lagoon. Fish is the main source of protein for villagers. [Papa, Sataua, Savai'i]

PAGE 33. Like a huge cobweb, the communally owned fishing net is draped about the *malae*, village green, to dry. [Leulumoega, Upolu]

PAGE 34. Two bonito canoes and their crews wait for the moment when they can clear the breakers and gain the open sea. If there is no *ava*, opening in the reef, several attempts are often necessary. [Foālalo, Savai'i]

PAGE 35. *Left.* A *masimasi*, dolphinfish, struggles. The fisherman deftly balances his outrigger canoe, paddling with one hand while he pulls in the line with the other. [Asau, Savai'i]
Right. A youthful fisherman prepares his coconut-twine noose for shark lassooing. At night, far beyond the reef, the coconut-shell rattle, seen leaning against the canoe, will be shaken to attract a shark. Bait is used to lure the shark's head into the noose, which is drawn tightly around his gills, and he is clubbed to death. [Falelima, Savai'i]

PAGE 36. *Left. Lama tofu* is night fishing with a lantern and a bushknife. The light attracts and blinds the sea life which is quickly dispatched with the knife. [Satufia, Savai'i]
Right. Atop a cliff, a fisherman takes aim at one of the large fish which feed among the rocks at twilight. [Falealupo, Savai'i]

PAGE 37. At the close of the day, the fishermen return. When the bonito are running, the men work all day in the open sea; upon reaching the shore, they share the fish among relatives and friends. [Vaisala, Savai'i]

PAGE 38. *Left.* A traditional Samoan house has no nails. Every part is fitted and then lashed together with coconut twine. [Tafuna, Tutuila]
Right. When a man wants a house for his family, he and his relatives and friends go into the forest, chop down the appropriate trees, and begin to fashion them into lumber. [Falealupo, Savai'i]

PAGE 39. *Left.* When a chief decides to build a *fale tele*, a guest house also used for council meetings, he has his talking chief contract with a skilled carpenter. In Samoa, the carpenter's ancient occupation is highly esteemed. Fine mats are presented, and the carpenter and his workmen are fed and housed while they work. Curved breadfruit beams are used to form the rounded ends of the house. [Tafuna, Tutuila]
Right. As much as five miles of twine is used to secure and make decorative patterns on the beams, posts, and rafters. [Fagamalo, Savai'i]

PAGE 40. Samoan houses are ideally suited to the climate—cool and open to the breezes, but secure from the elements when the woven blinds are let down. The size of the house and the height of the platform it is built on are related to the importance of the owner's title. [Falealupo, Savai'i]

PAGE 41. *Left.* The weaving of the roofing thatch from sugarcane or palm leaves is the work of women. Girls learn this skill from childhood by watching their mothers at work. [Satoalepai, Savai'i]
Top. A special house was built for the construction of this long boat, or *fautasi*, which measures eighty-six feet from bow to stern. Such a project is a huge undertaking for a village; some fifteen carpenters were housed and fed during the months it took to complete this boat. Dozens of men will be needed to row it. The village built it to compete in the Independence races. [Falealupo, Savai'i]
Bottom. A carpenter skilled at woodcarving works on a kava bowl. The dried and pounded root of the kava tree is mixed with water in this bowl. Kava is served at welcoming ceremonies and before the village council begins its deliberations. [Asau, Savai'i]

PAGE 42. *Left.* A taro leaf stretched across the top of a container makes a good palette for tattooing dye. In the past, the dye was made from morning dew and the specially prepared soot of burnt candlenuts. Today it is made of water and lampblack. [Falelatai, Upolu]
Right. An enameled basin imported from Japan holds a set of heirloom tattooing instruments. The comb is carved from the tusk of a wild boar, the flange from the shell of a sea turtle, and the handle is of polished wood. All are lashed together with fine coconut twine. A selection of combs of different widths permits variation in the patterning. [Sili, Savai'i]

PAGE 43. The *tufuga tatau*, tattoo artist, with his apprentice and helpers, patterns the bodies of two young men in the traditional marks of manliness. Villagers crowd the house to watch the proceedings and encourage the young men with songs to distract them from the painful ordeal which usually requires at least a week to complete. [Sili, Savai'i]

PAGE 44. *Left.* The *tufuga*'s apprentice carefully observes every detail of the master's skill. [Sili, Savai'i]
Right. The apprentice assists by stretching the skin to a smooth working surface. Holding the knee steady with his foot, the tattooist taps in the line marking the lower limit of the tattoo. The full pattern covers the body from the lower chest to just below the knees. [Sili, Savai'i]

PAGE 45. Each evening the young men being tattooed bathe together in the village stream. In earlier times coconut water was sprinkled on a man when his tattoo was completed. Once patterned, he is able to prepare certain ceremonial foods, eat a particular fish, and is the preferred kava server. Possession of a tattoo is a firm step toward the acquisition of a title. [Sili, Savai'i]

Children at Work and Play

Over one-half the population of Western Samoa is under sixteen years of age, and an extensive school system offers education from the primary grades through university entrance. Both public and parochial schools are found in villages throughout the islands; secondary schools tend to be located near the capital. The educational system is patterned after that of New Zealand's, but with distinctive Samoan modifications.

By observing and helping, children learn most of the skills of village life. They are rarely, however, under pressure to either learn or perform tasks according to a rigid schedule. Much of their work is interspersed with play, using as toys whatever is at hand. Children are quite free to eat and even sleep in homes other than their own; ultimately, if they wish, they can go and live with a favorite relative.

PAGE 46. *Left.* Each school has its own uniform. School buildings are decorated with flowers which the children bring every day. [Satoalepai/Fagamalo, Savai'i]
Right. School boys fold their arms and bow their heads for morning prayer. All schools in Western Samoa, both government and parochial, elementary and secondary, begin the day with a prayer, a hymn, and the national anthem. [Satoalepai/Fagamalo, Savai'i]

PAGE 47. Youngsters are taught at an early age to set out their lessons neatly. [Satoalepai/Fagamalo, Savai'i]

PAGE 48. *Left.* Pupils vie with one another to answer their teacher's questions. Younger children sit on mats during the lesson. Most teachers in the village schools receive their preparation at the government's Teachers Training College in Apia. [Satoalepai/Fagamalo, Savai'i]
Center. The lessons on the blackboard spell out the English words for the colors and reenforce what is taught at home about personal cleanliness. From the early school years on, both English and Samoan are used in the classroom. [Lalomanu, Upolu]
Right. A youngster, still wearing his village school uniform, makes a toy of a discarded bicycle wheel under his older brother's supervision. [Satoalepai, Savai'i]

PAGE 49. *Left.* Children in Samoa do many kinds of work to help the family. Even little ones perform useful tasks like fetching burning charcoal to make a fire. It is often difficult to draw the line between the work and play of younger children, such as these boys washing horses in the sea. [Satufia, Savai'i]
Right. Village children cross a coconut-log bridge on their way home with bundles of sugarcane leaves to be used for thatching. [Safa'i, Savai'i]

PAGE 50. *Left.* A coconut tree becomes the village grandstand from which to watch a rugby match among older brothers. [Fagamalo, Savai'i]
Right. Schoolmates watch intently from the sidelines. [Apia, Upolu]

PAGE 51. The rubgy teams jump for the ball. [Apia, Upolu]

PAGE 52. *Top.* A school girl and her brother test the strength of a captive cricket by giving him progressively heavier coral chips to hold. [Satoalepai, Savai'i]
Bottom. A sandy front yard makes a fine hopscotch court. The rules of the game are phenomenally complicated. [Satoalepai, Savai'i]

PAGE 53. *Left.* Almost every village has a volleyball and net. In the early evening, after their work is done, the young people gather to play or watch. [Papa, Sataua, Savai'i]
Right. The other game played in nearly every village is cricket. All that is needed is a concrete "pitch," a heavy Samoan bat, a homemade rubber ball, and enough strength to put them all together. The player at bat is often encouraged by songs and dances performed by his teammates, who also do their best to distract the opposition. [Satufia, Savai'i]

Ceremonies and Celebrations

The ceremonial life of Samoa is rich. Ceremonies are usually accompanied by the drinking of kava, the giving of speeches, the distribution of fine mats, and celebrations of feasting, singing, and dancing. Ceremonies mark occasions of great joy or sadness. Guests are welcomed and council meetings are begun with the kava ceremony. The year after a chief dies, his title is honored in the lagi. A saofa'i is held when a title is assumed. These, and many other ceremonies, unite distant branches of families and provide opportunities to familiarize and solidify relations.

History and legends are often reenacted as part of a ceremony, and it is on such occasions that chiefs especially embroider their speech with proverbial sayings.

PAGE 54. *Left.* An orator, or talking chief, bearing the symbols of his office, the *to'oto'o*, staff, and *fue*, flywhisk, and wearing a tapa lavalava, delivers a speech to a village gathering. [Safune, Savai'i]
Right. A matai on his way to a church dedication carries an armload of kava sticks, the root end of which is used to prepare the ceremonial drink. Taro, on litters, foreground, is ready to be taken to the feast. The local bus brings one of many loads of guests right to the center of the village. [Sagone, Savai'i]

PAGE 55. In the high ceremony of *'ava fa'a tupu*, king's kava, the drink is prepared outside the house rather than inside as is ordinarily the custom. The drink is mixed by the *manaia*, a specially titled young man, who here strains the liquid with fibers of the *fau*, wild hibiscus. The *manaia* wears a headdress of bleached human hair, decorative feathers, shells, and beads. On these occasions, the honored guest is presented with fire, fine mats, and food. [Lefaga'oali'i, Savai'i]

PAGE 56. *Top.* Fine mats previously collected from relatives of the family involved in the ceremony are displayed and redistributed. In the particular ceremony, *lagi*, shown, the family of a deceased high chief presented fine mats to all the talking chiefs of the district in order to maintain the dignity and respect of the title and to reaffirm their relationships with the orators. [Lefaga'oali'i, Savai'i]
Bottom. At the *umusaga*, a ceremony celebrating the completion of a building, the relatives of the owner strengthen their relationships by contributing fine mats, tapa cloths, and money toward the carpenters' pay. Each mat and its donor are carefully recorded. [Lalomanu, Upolu]
Right. As the ceremony continues, orators who have already received their fine mats carefully note the recipients of the remaining mats. [Lefaga'oali'i, Savai'i]

PAGE 57. *Left.* His shoulders respectfully draped with a banana leaf *ula*, necklace, a young man prepares *fa'ausi*, hot taro dumplings made with coconut cream and carmelized sugar, served in individual baskets. [Lalomanu, Upolu]
Center. Boys and young men are responsible for the heavy cooking done in the ground oven, or *umu*. The food, placed directly on heated lava rocks, is covered with leaves and mats and left to cook for approximately an hour. [Sagone, Savai'i]
Right. Over one hundred pigs, partially cooked to facilitate ceremonial division, were distributed at this particular celebration. The families who received the meat later completed the cooking. Traditional rules prescribe the division and distribution of the meat; for example, the loins to the high chief, the neck to the talking chiefs, the head of the pig to the cooks. [Sagone, Savai'i]

PAGE 58. *Left.* An elderly chief returning home from a ceremony is followed by his small grandson who carries a fine mat carefully wrapped in a tapa cloth. [Lelepa, Savai'i]
Right. Most of the food is not consumed at the feast, but is put aside in baskets to be taken home. This man is paddling home with a keg of salted beef. [Safune, Savai'i]

PAGE 59. *Left.* This village women's group, the *aualuma*, performs songs and dances in uniforms of red and white, which they have made especially for this celebration. [Papa, Sataua, Savai'i]
Right. A young man performs a siva, a traditional Samoan dance, during an evening *fia fia*, party. Visitors and hosts sit in groups across from each other and challenge one another in the presentation of songs, dances, and jokes. [Papa, Sataua, Savai'i]

PAGE 60. *Left.* Wearing a *titi*, a girdle of feathers, a young man performs a dance of rapid movements and rhythmical slaps on the chest, arms, and legs. Custom dictates that men dance bare chested. [Apia, Upolu]
Right. During the Independence celebrations each June, villages compete with one another in their performances. [Apia, Upolu]

PAGE 61. In the older style of dancing, formalized hand and arm movements are executed while sitting or standing. Some of the best dancing is done by the elderly. This woman is taking part in a mass dance called the *sasa*. [Apia, Upolu]

PAGE 62. *Top.* The *taupou*, titled village hostess, wearing her spectacular headdress of bleached human hair, mirrors, and brightly colored sticks and feathers, leads the *aualuma*, village women's group, in a performance. [Apia, Upolu]
Bottom. Seated for the *sasa*, a woman claps her hands and gestures to the rhythm beaten by her crossed legs. As many as several hundred dancers may perform the *sasa* in unison. [Apia, Upolu]
Center. To the beat of sticks upon rolled mats, the leader of a women's committee directs the singing and clapping. [Sataua, Savai'i]
Right. The songleader's precisionlike positions and movements indicate the rhythm and exactly when various types of claps, hollow or flat, are to punctuate the song. [Sataua, Savai'i]

PAGE 63. At dawn, five miles out beyond the reef, village *fautasi*, longboats, begin their race toward the shore in a competition that climaxes the annual celebration marking the independence in January 1962 of the first Polynesian nation in modern times. These crews are nearing the finish line. [Apia, Upolu]

Religion

Christianity was formally introduced in Samoa in 1830 by John Williams of the London Missionary Society. So rapidly was it integrated into the culture that by 1840 virtually all Samoans were professed Christians. A few years later they were training their own pastors and sending missionaries to the Solomon Islands, the New Hebrides, and New Guinea. There are three main churches in Samoa—the Congregational Christian church of Samoa (formerly the London Missionary Society), the Catholic church, and the Methodist church. There are also several smaller groups, such as the Latter Day Saints and the Seventh Day Adventists. Church plays a very significant part in the lives of the people.

PAGE 64. *Top.* A large hollow log, *lali,* is used by some churches to call people to meetings, the choir to practice, or children to pastor's school. [Satufia, Savai'i]
Bottom. It is not unusual to find two or three large churches in a village of three hundred people. If a new building is desired, the matai, who often act as church elders, select the style; the people raise the money to buy the necessary materials; and the village carpenters recreate the structure from a picture or according to their own design. [Piula, Upolu]
Right. Each Sunday, almost the entire village turns out for both morning and afternoon services. Seating arrangements follow village social patterns, with the chiefs in one part of the church, and untitled men, women, boys, and girls in their own sections. On special occasions the women decorate the building with chandeliers of flowers. Accompanied by a pump organ, the choir leads the congregation in intricate hymns. [Satoalepai, Savai'i]

PAGE 65. *Left.* The head of a women's church organization opens a district meeting with a Bible passage. [Satoalepai, Savai'i]
Right. Sunday afternoons are reserved for rest and religious study. Here a high chief, an ali'i, reads his Bible before the afternoon church service. [Satoalepai, Savai'i]

PAGE 66. The pastor and his wife hold school several times each week. Older children bring their younger brothers and sisters. It is not uncommon for a child of five or six to know the alphabet and do simple arithmetic before beginning the village school. [Satoalepai, Savai'i]

PAGE 67. *Top.* The pastor's wife, aided by a magnifying glass as she follows along, listens to a child read aloud from the Bible. Polynesians, renowned for their ability to recite genealogies, are equally adept at remembering hundreds of hymns and Bible verses. [Satoalepai, Savai'i]
Bottom Left. On the second Sunday of October of each year, the usual social customs are reversed. It is the parents who serve the children at the meal instead of the other way around. The children also get new white clothes for church and other gifts. [Utuali'i, Upolu]
Bottom Right. A village wedding combines much of Western and Samoan traditions. Often the bride is given several wedding gowns by different parts of the family. Consequently she may have a dress for her marriage, one for the feasting, and another for the dancing. [Avao, Savai'i]

PAGE 68. *Left.* Most Samoans believe strongly in an afterlife. Often very old people, unafraid of and completely prepared for their deaths, will sleep in or near their coffins. [Satufia, Savai'i]
Right. When it comes, death is met with equanimity. Friends and relatives visit the family, and present them with fine mats as a sign of respect. later, the mats are redistributed among the guests, and a communal feast is held. [Falevao, Upolu]

PAGE 69. A youth comforts his younger adopted brother as they stand at the edge of their father's grave. [Fagamalo, Savai'i]

Evening

As dusk falls, the crickets cry, and young people, strolling after their work is done, return to their homes. Preparations have begun for the evening meal. When the village church bell, or the conch shell, announces the time for family prayers, the villagers pause and make their evening service. Many of the children go to the pastor's home and join his family for prayer.

After the meal, people relax and perhaps have a massage, visit one another, and discuss the village day.

PAGE 70. *Left.* The lanterns are lit each evening before prayers and the second meal of the day. [Leulumoega, Upolu]
Right. The whole family gathers for the evening prayers, which are conducted by the matai of the family. Hymns are sung, a passage from the Bible is read, and a prayer is offered. [Falealupo, Savai'i]

PAGE 71. A young son leans against his father during the evening prayers. The proverb "Pray for both Tuna and Fata" refers to the petition of a young man long ago who prayed for the lives of both his cousins who had mortally wounded one another in an argument. [Sili, Savai'i]

PAGE 72. A chief sleeps on his wooden pillow. Formerly these pillows were made of bamboo logs several feet long, and served a number of sleepers at the same time. The free circulation of air is ideal. [Sili, Savai'i]

PAGE 73. The Southern Cross, the lovely kite-shaped constellation of the Southern Hemisphere, has been made famous by stories of the South Seas. It figures prominently in the flag of Western Samoa. [Satoalepai, Savai'i]

Epilogue

PAGE 74. The small islands of Nu'utele and Nu'ulua seen from the coast of Aleipata. [southeast coast of Upolu]

PAGE 75. Houses of a village are clustered like birds' nests at the base of the forested slopes of Mauga Silisili (elevation 6,095 feet). [Matavai, Savai'i]

PAGE 76. A fisherman crosses the lagoon to an offshore island where canoes are often beached for easy access to sea or lagoon. The island is a favorite night fishing spot. [Safa'i, Savai'i]

PAGE 77. The sun, which sets rapidly in the tropics, slips beneath the horizon, but its rays briefly linger. [Falealupo, Savai'i]

PAGE 78. Day's end, and a small group of people return to their offshore island home. [Manono Uta and Manono Island]

PAGE 79. [Tafatafa, Upolu]

Proverbs Cited

Page 4. **Ia lafoia i le alogalu.** Dr. E. Schultz, *Proverbial Expressions of the Samoans*, Brother Herman, trans., Polynesian Paperbacks no. 1 (Wellington, New Zealand: Polynesian Society, 1965), 296.

Page 6. **Ua aofia i le futiafu e tasi.** Schultz, 354.

Sa matou tu'u la'au mai nei. Schultz, 114.

Page 8. **Tolona e le masina matua.** Reverend George Brown, "Proverbs, Phrases, and Similes of the Samoans," *Report of the Fourteenth Meeting of the Australasian Association for the Advancement of Science*, Sydney, 1914, 69.

Ua solo le lāvalima. Schultz, 166.

Page 9. **Ua pulapula a la goto.** Reverend George Pratt, *Pratt's Grammar and Dictionary of the Samoan Language*, 4th ed., J. E. Newell, ed. (Malua, Western Samoa: Malua Printing Press, 1960), 94.

'O le isi le momo'o. Pratt, 30.

Page 11. **O faiva 'aulelei.** Schultz, 210.

Page 12. **Ua sanisani fa'amanuao.** Pratt, 103.

Page 14. **Ua se vai ma lauta'ele.** Schultz, 332.

Page 15. **Taule'ale'a usu mai.** Brown, 150.

Page 16. **Na o le taeao o faiva.** Schultz, 530.

Page 20. **E tasi 'ae afe.** Schultz, 161.

Page 23. **Ia tupu i se fusi.** Schultz, 189.

Page 25. **Ia lua'i lou le 'ulu taumamao.** Brown, 71.

Ua vela lana umu i lo tatou nu'u. Pratt, 42.

Page 26. **Ua tofo i tino matagi lelei.** Pratt, 129.

Māmā i avega si'i. Brown, 79.

Fā le taeao e le afiafi. Schultz, 198.

Page 29. **Ua penapena i tua o tai i'a.** Schultz, 70.

Mālō le 'onosa'i. Common saying.

O le i'a a tautai e alu i le fa'alolo. Schultz, 22.

Page 30. **Ua a'e a'e lea manu ua ulu.** Personal communication.

Fa'atoetoe le muli o le ola. Schultz, 202.

Page 33. **O le fa'afiti a tautai.** Brown, 198.

O le upega e tautau, 'ae fagota. Pratt, 39.

Page 35. **Ia fili i le tai se agava'a.** Pratt, 14.

Ua logo le na i ama, logo le na i atea. Schultz, 492.

O le malie ma le tu'u malie. Schultz, 34.

Page 36. **O upu matatutupa.** Brown, 134.

Page 37. **Ua sau le va'a na tiu tau mai i le va'a na tau.** Personal communication.

Page 39. **Ua logo 'ese'ese fa'amea vilivili.** Schultz, 157.

Ia ta'amilo pea ma tautala. Schultz, 139.

Page 41. **Ua mua ane lava se fale.** Schultz, 133.

Ia oloolo pitova'a. Schultz, 150.

Page 42. **Pula ū.** Personal communication.

Pages 42, 44, 45. The tattoo song. From Brother Herman's translation of Augustin Kramer, *Die Samoan Inseln*, Stuttgart, 1902, mimeographed.

Page 48. **Ua pipili tia 'ae mamao ala.** Schultz, 92.

Page 49. **E tele a ululau.** Pratt, 41.

Page 50. **Ua uō uō foa.** Schultz, 328.

Ua vilivili fa'amanu o matagi. Pratt, 130.

Page 52. **Ua lauiloa e pili ma sē.** Pratt, 58.

Page 53. **Ua leai se ulu e ala.** Schultz, 501.

Page 54. **E pala ma'a, 'ae le pala 'upu.** Pratt, 89.

Page 55. **Ua le po malaē.** Schultz, 506.

Page 56. **E o'u le asō; 'ae o oe taeao.** Schultz, 423.

Musumusu a puiali'i. Schultz, 521.

Page 57. **Ua mu le lima tapa le i'ofi.** Pratt, 56.

O le sala e tau'ave i le fofoga. Schultz, 529.

Page 61. **Ua vela le fala.** Schultz, 165.

Page 62. **Ua liua le tua ma lealo.** Brown, 139.

Page 64. **Ia uluulu matāfolau.** Pratt, 37.

Page 65. **Fa'avae i le Atua Samoa.** In Western Samoa's constitution; common knowledge.

Page 68. **Ua felāta'i le la ma le sami.** Brown, 127.

O le la'au e tu, 'ae ōia. Pratt, 33.

Page 69. **Ua tagi le fatu ma le ele'ele.** Brown, 153.

Page 70. **Tagi o alisi.** Common saying.

Tāla lua Tuna ma Fata. Schultz, 385.

Page 72. **Ua tofa i vai, 'ae ala i 'ai.** Pratt, 20.

Page 74. **Samoa e le galo atu.** Samoan farewell song; common knowledge.

Page 75. **Ua leai se manu e ōlo.** Schultz, 89.

Page 77. **Tuaoi afā ma maninoa.** Brown, 42.

Ua lāolāo le sami. Schultz, 284.

Page 78. **O le mavaega nai le tai e fetaia'i i i'u o gafa.** Schultz, 430.

DATE DUE

GAYLORD			PRINTED IN U.S.A.